There's nothing as lovely as a…

Lowcountry Christmas!

From Williamsburg and Norfolk… cascading down the Outer Banks through inland rural and beach and sound areas…on to Wilmington and the Crystal Coast…down to Charleston, Beaufort, Bluffton…into Gullah Geechee country…to Savannah and beyond—this entire swath of Lowcountry coastland is a treasure trove of holiday history, recipes, events, music, and more. Learn about the sights and sounds, the scents, the remarkable food from slave to colonial to contemporary eras. From rice, cotton, and tobacco plantations to swank soirees, learn about the lovely Lowcountry traditions from times past.

"It makes you want to take to the road to see and taste and experience such a kind of Christmas!"

Lowcountry CHRISTMAS A to Z

Includes Recipes!

Carole Marsh Longmeyer

Published by Gallopade International,
Peachtree City, Georgia.

For permissions or author interview, contact Gallopade at
800-536-2438.

Lowcountry Christmas Team:

Susan Van Denhende, Graphic Design
Jon McKenna, Gallopade New Product Development
Janice Baker, Editor
Glenda Harris, Copyeditor
John Hanson, Art Director
Tommy Dean, Printing and Binding

Measurements: In the past, Lowcountry cooks seldom bothered with precise measuring c.s and spoons. Even today, thankfully, you can find quaint measuring tools that read things like smidgen, pinch, dash, tad, drop, or such. In this book, unless exceedingly necessary, I have adhered to these charming, old-fashioned measurements. Note: "Receipts" is what they called recipes.

Also by Carole Marsh Longmeyer

A Carolina Christmas

The White House Christmas Mystery

The Secret Christmas Potpourri &
Tussie Mussie Story Kit

The Epiphany Surprise Christmas Cake
Story Kit

The Chinese Fortune Cookie Christmas
Story & Ornament Kit

The Victorian Crazy Christmas Cobweb
Party Kit

Christmas Recipes from the Past

Savannah Night Before Christmas

Dedicated to my family: Each December we celebrate two birthdays, Christmas Eve, Christmas, and a wedding anniversary!

 # Table of Contents

Introduction...............................13
A-Z..17
Recipes.....................................95
Bibliography..........................131

Lowcountry CHRISTMAS A to Z

Carole Marsh Longmeyer

Introduction

A Lowcountry Christmas is like no other! I can't say exactly why, except that you often have to blink your eyes and think hard if you are in the past or the present when you are celebrating Christmas in the Lowcountry!

Why is that? Because, just for a few examples from some of my favorite memories:

• Churches that date back to the 1800s (or earlier!) festooned with natural greenery and holly berries, awash in the glow of beeswax candle flames, smelling of warm cider and molasses cookies, and sounding ancient bells and hymns.

• Mansions on the Battery of Charleston gleaming in holiday finery for home tours where you are greeted by rosy-faced folks in period costumes. You can wander gaslit streets of Christmas past!

•An "Old Bull" Ephipany celebration on the Outer Banks that dates back 400 years. If you're lucky, it will snow on the steaming oysters they serve!

•Long back road rides along the sea from Norfolk to Jacksonville with detours to waterside villages and towns with wreaths on lighthouses, authentic craft festivals, and holiday food from colonial Lemon Chess Pie to Chocolate Trifle, and so much more.

I could go on and on, but all will appear in this book. Still, just writing this my mind is sugarplumed with thoughts of Tryon Palace, the Beaufort waterfront, Wormsloe in Savannah, and quieter venues such as shops selling corn husk dolls…cafes with Tudor décor serving hot clam chowder and hushpuppies…

and old slave quarters on rice plantations with their own unique celebrations.

In fact, I might have just discovered that I'm a Christmasholic? When I am reminded of all the beautiful places that my husband, Bob, and I have seen in the Lowcountry during the holiday season, I marvel at how wonderful it all is. Too wonderful to leave just to December, so enjoy this book in July, if you will.

Yes, there are beautiful Christmases everywhere, but somehow, to me, the Lowcountry Christmas is best: the history, the nostalgia, the legend, lore, and so much more. Now why didn't I think to drink eggnog when I was writing this book? Hmm…never too late!

Merrie Olde Christmas, always, readers!

Carole Marsh Longmeyer
Beaufort, South Carolina

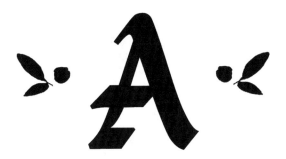

A Sweet Christmas: It's not Christmas in the Lowcountry without homemade divinity, pralines, fudge, peanut brittle, rum balls, caramel, toffee, sea foam, candied fruit peel, saltwater taffy, and more. In Savannah, both River Street Sweets and the Savannah Candy Kitchen stay busy making, selling, and shipping holiday candy around the country. In Beaufort, we have the Chocolate Tree!

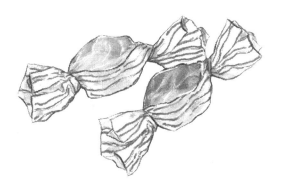

B

Bakeries: You'll never lack for red and green sweets for the Lowcountry holidays. Frozen s'mores, anyone? Back in the Day Bakery, in the Starland area of Savannah, specializes in white holiday cakes frosted with red poinsettia flowers. Other popular baked goods available during the season include chocolate-covered cherry cookies, ladyfingers, cheese straws, pinwheels with mayhaw jelly, gingerbread with lemon glaze, lace cookies, eggnog lb. cake, and mile high red velvet cake.

Big House Christmas: Christmas on a Lowcountry plantation was a family affair! Relatives came for Thanksgiving and stayed in the house until after Christmas. Children decorated the tree with paper chains and fancy ornaments from Germany or England. Most children only received one gift, so it was very special! A boy might get a knife or a ball. A girl might get a china doll.

Birds of Christmas: The Lowcountry is home to a wide variety of land and shore birds. Many people enjoy creating winter feasts for local and migrating birds such as the house finch, goldfinch, white pelican, blue jay, brown thrasher, brown-headed cowbird, great blue heron, American kestrel, European starling, chipping sparrow, red-shouldered hawk, cardinal, bald eagle, yellow-rumped warbler, eastern bluebird, ruby-crowned kinglet, tufted titmouse, tundra swan, and more. Take your binoculars to the beach and to the many wildlife management areas and participate in a winter bird count!

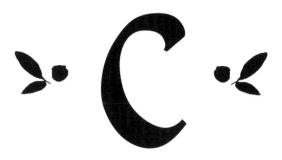

Cakes: From time out of mind, Christmas was all about cakes: coconut, red velvet peppermint, gingerbread cakes, pumpkin praline, hot chocolate cake, spicy banana, fruit, persimmon, mincemeat, hickory nut, and many more, often with as many as sixteen layers, and all frosted as thick as any snowfall.

Carolina Custom: Says day breaks twice on Old Christmas, with the poke stalks and hop vines up early, while at midnight the barnyard animals would kneel and pray.

Carolina Soldier's Christmas

Christmas is a hard day for all soldiers in all wars. In the past, Christmas for a Carolina soldier was very difficult. First, he was away from home. Second, he might even be fighting on Christmas Day. Third, it was usually really cold! He might enjoy a drink of whiskey in his tent at the end of the day.

Christmas was brighter for soldiers at an army post. They might have a get-together. They might have a special ration of whiskey or a poker game to pass the time. Still, they missed the Christmas they would have at home.

Army officers sometimes had their families living with them. Army wives often arranged parties at Christmas. They looked forward to them all year long! It was a time to have fun.

The railroad brought special food and drink for the Christmas celebrations. The railroad also brought gifts for Army children from relatives far away. Christmas was much more cheerful when families were together!

Today, North and South Carolina soldiers are spread out all over the world-in times of peace and war. We should always remember them at Christmas. They love to get cards and letters!

Christmas Trees Colors: While we generally associate red, white, and green with Christmas, Lowcountry homes, great and small, add additional color schemes to the holiday season. Simple, coastal cottages favored natural greenery and the sand-color of shells of all kinds. Grandiose mansions entertained with bright yellow walls (or wallpaper), beautiful blues from marine blue to seafoam or even peppermint pink walls, upholstery, and decorations.

City Decorations: Nothing is prettier than the Lowcountry mansions of Charleston and Savannah adorned in their Christmas finery. Central to this is the pineapple, a traditional symbol of welcome. Fresh pine garlands are swathed around gaslights and front doors boast of displays of apples, pine cones, and more evergreens. Other decorations may include Spanish moss, mistletoe, sea whips, Star of Bethlehem, coral, jasmine, magnolia leaves, topiary, viburnum branches, pomegranates, key limes, kumquats, white lilies, palm fronds, candy cane camellias, and more. From the beach come seashells and starfish. Personally I love a tiny tree with white lights and white sand dollars, starfish, seashells, and Spanish Moss.

Christmas Greenery: You could always count on Lowcountry houses to be festooned, indoors and out, with natural greenery, such as smilax, holly, magnolia, pine cones, berries, and if you are lucky (rarely in the Lowcountry) a dusting of snow.

Christmas Trees: While the Virginia scrub pine seems born to be the Christmas tree, in the Lowcountry you can also find white pine, Norfolk pine, Leland cypress, Eastern red cedar, and more. Christmas tree farms and stands selling trees abound in the Lowcountry. Families also trek to farms to enjoy cutting their own trees. Christmas hay wagon rides are also popular.

Cider: Hot cider or wassail is popular during Christmas caroling. While there are many recipes, to me the best is the most organic apple juice you can get steeped with plenty of cloves overnight.

Cookies: What is Christmas without cookies? Popular in the Lowcountry from colonial days onward: icebox cookies, gingerbread, molasses cookies, mincemeat squares, anise cookies, sugar cookies, thumbprints, and many more. My favorite are stained glass cookies, where colored candies sprinkled into the dough melt into see-thru colored squares to crunch on.

Country Christmas
by Roy Taylor

The fireworks have arrived at the freight station and the boys have to find a way to get them home, even if the wagon has to be driven to town. Every year the neighborhood boys get together and order fireworks from far-away places. And the old neighborhood sparkles at night. Sky rockets, Roman candles, torpedoes, strings of tiny firecrackers, spit devils, sparklers—they are all included. Children get most of their Christmas spending money from scrap cotton that is sold at the gin. But first things first. Go to the woodpile, boys, with your hatchet and hammer. Get the sack of black walnuts and turn a round piece of wood on end and crack the nuts on it. Turn them at an angle, so there will be large pieces of meat instead of mush. Pick out the pecans, girls, plenty of them. They'll be used in a lot of things, and don't try cracking them with a flat iron. It'll mash them to pieces. And don't try to crack the hard ones with your teeth. Check on all the ingredients in the pantry to see if anything is missing. Yeah, vanilla flavoring is about out and some will have to be bought. Nutmeg is sufficient. Spice supply adequate. Ginger a plenty. Chocolate's a mite low. Add that to the list. Coconuts sound all right from shaking them.

Go out to the pasture and kill that pig, boys. Dress him out and get him ready for a good portion— will be baked Christmas Eve. The oven will be reserved for that 35-lb. turkey gobbler all night so he'll be tender enough to fall off the bone Christmas Day. Find paper sacks to place over him so he won't get too brown while cooking. Grate that coconut, girls, and be careful with that grater. You could ruin a finger and grate a hunk of flesh if you don't watch what you're doing. Measure out a sifter full of flour for each bowl and don't bother about measuring out lard in a cup. Takes too long. Dip down in the lard stand and come up with a good-sized chunk and do the same for every cake. And remember—you want a cake to be good and short. Now, boys, pluck out the feathers. Save the part of the wing that ain't good for eating.

Makes good dusters for the house. That little bit of meat and gristle will dry out and they're good for dusting off the furniture. Reckon there will be enough to feed 'em all? It would be a shame not to have enough. It's a hard job, getting ready for Christmas. No end to the work, but what would it be without all this? Been too busy to even know what the weather's like. Looks snowy, but don't count on that, for snow just stays away at Christmas. Ice was two-inches thick on watering troughs this morning. Will be as cold tonight. All the folks will be coming in pretty soon. There'll sure be a crowd around. But it seems just like Christmas.

Sharecroppers: The Way We Really Were, Roy Taylor, 1984

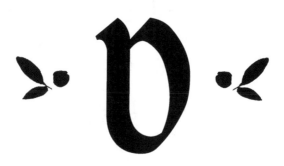

De Birth Story in Gullah

Een dat time, Caesar Augustus been de big leada, de emperor ob de Roman people. E make a law een all de town eed de wold weh he habe tority, say "Ebrybody haffa go ta town fa county by de hed an write down e nyame." Dis been de fus time dey count by de hed, same time Cyrenius de gobna ob Syria country. So den, ebrybody gone fa count by de hed, ta e own town weh e ole people been bon.

Now Joseph same fashion gone from Nazrut town een Galilee. E trabel ta de town nyame Betlam een Judea, weh de ole people leada, King David, been bon. Joseph gone dey cause e blongst ta David fambly. E gone fa count by de hed an Mary gone long wid um. She gage fa married um. An Mary been spectin. Same time wen dey been dey, time come fa Mary gone een.

She habe boy chile, e fusbon. E wrop um open clothe wa been teah eenta leetle strip an lay um een a trough, de box weh feed de cow an oda animal. Cause Mary and Joseph beena stay weh de animal sleep. Dey ain't been no room fa dem enside de bodin house.

Now some shephud been dey een de fiel dat night time. Dey beena stay dey, da mind dey sheep. Den one angel ob de Lawd appeah ta um. De night time done lightin op jes like day clean broad. Dat de glory ob de Lawd wa shine bout um. Cause ob dat, de shephud mos scaid ta det. Bot de angel tell um say, "Mus don't feah! A habe good nywes. Cause ob dis nyews, oona gwine rejoice. All de people gwine rejoice tommuch.

Cause A come fa tell oona, 'Right now, dis day, a Sabior done bon fa oona. He de Promise Chile, Christ, de Lawd. An e bon een David town!' A gwine tell oona whatoona gwine see dey. Cause ob dat, oona gwine know A done tell oona de trut. Oona gwine find de childe wrop op een clothe wa been teah eenta leetle strip and e been led-down een a trough."

All ob a sudden, a heap ob oda angel from heaben been longside dat angel. Dey all da praise God, say, "Leh we gee glory ta Gad een de mos high heaven."

"Leh dey be peace ta dem een de wol wa habe Bod fabor!"

Luke 2:1-14, from "De Good Nyews Bout Jedus Christ Wa Luke Write," published in 1994 by American Bible Society.

Dolls: Like Christmas morning today, the Lowcountry past was filled with dreams of dolls beneath the tree, ranging from corn husk dolls, wooden soldiers, dolls riding horses, rag dolls, sock dolls, calico dolls, and all that dolls might need, such as tables, chairs, beds, rockers, cribs, and even toy boats to sail and toy horses to ride.

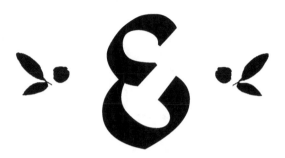

Expensive oranges: "Oranges are five dollars apiece — if you can get them!" wrote Mary Boykin Chesnut of Camden, SC, in her 1863 Christmas diary entry. Of course, all fruit was precious and expensive in the South in the month of December!

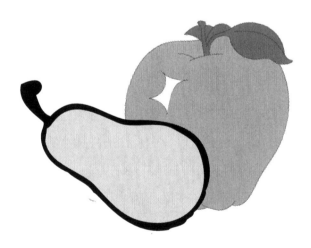

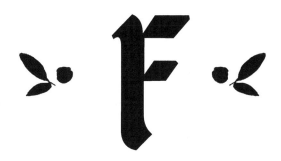

Famous Folks and Places: While you might not be able to actually visit all of these, Lowcountry lanes have many secrets, such as the former winter retreat of Henry Ford on the Ogeechee River, just outside Savannah. A former rice plantation, this property is now the star of a beautiful island of fine homes. In South Carolina, you can go to Yemassee and pass by an authentic Frank Lloyd Wright home with all ninety-degree angles.

Favorite Lowcountry Holiday Foods: Sweet potato biscuits with ham, steamed stone craw claws, blue crab bisque, shrimp cocktail, and much more. See the recipes at the end of this book!

Firecrackers: Have long been a part of a Lowcountry Christmas. Some believe the habit originated when early settlers sent holiday greetings to fellow colonists by shooting off firearms; others say the noise was first created to drive away evil spirits.

First Flight: One of the most historic December events on the Lowcountry coast was Orville and Wilbur Wright's first flight over the sand dunes in North Carolina on December 17, 1903. My husband and I belonged for years to the Man Will Never Fly Society. While winter raged on the coast, this was always a merry celebration in honor of the twelve seconds that changed the world!

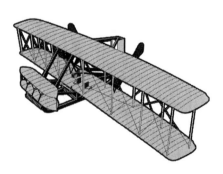

flying High on Christmas

Christmastime was a busy time for two brothers in 1903. They weren't thinking about presents, decorating a tree, or Christmas dinner. They were thinking about one of the most important inventions in history!

Orville and Wilbur Wright made Lowcountry history on December 17, 1903. It was a bitterly cold day on the coast of North Carolina. Puddles of water on the sand had frozen during the night. The wind howled along at 27 miles per hour. Orville lay face-down on the bottom wing of the flying machine built by the brothers. The flyer began to move forward and took off into the sky. It only flew for

12 seconds, but that was enough! The Wright Brothers had made history!

The Wright brothers made two more flights that day. Then they headed home for a very merry Christmas!

Fountains: One of the prettiest holiday sites in the Lowcountry are the many wedding cake-like fountains adorned with greenery and red ribbons. Not to miss, especially, is Forsyth Square in Savannah, the largest National Historic Landmark District in the United States. Each of its twenty-two squares are uniquely decked-out for Christmas, as well. Home tours and merchant open houses abound throughout the season. One delicious annual event is the bed and breakfast open house, where you get to see inside the mansions and sample some of their delicious high tea offerings. Churches, cathedrals, and synagogues are often open for viewing.

Fruitcake: Some Lowcountry cooks swear the secret to a great fruitcake is to bake it in October, wrap it in cheesecloth, and drizzle it with peach brandy once a week until Christmas!

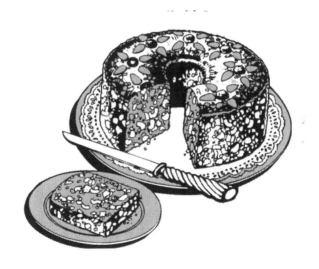

Goodie String: If you visited a rural Lowcountry family at Christmas, you might be offered a treat from the "goodie string." Here's how to make your own for your visitors:

Take 3 feet of mailing cord. On the cord, string the following (tie a big knot in one end and put an apple on first):

Apples
Popcorn balls
Cookies
Cotton balls tied with red yarn
"Baggies" of pecans or peanuts
Small toys or gifts

When you fill the string, tie a simple bow on top and hang it on the back of the front door. Each guest can pick the next "goodie" from the string!

Grandma's Christmas: Any child's holiday is made more special when it involves an "over the river and through the woods" trip to grandmother's house! The only hills in the Lowcountry are sand dunes, of course, but the trek down some long, straight sandy lane to the sea makes for a special Christmas morning. The scent of dew-frosted holly berries, yaupon tea simmering in the kettle, benne wafers just coming out of the oven, the salted air, smoke from driftwood in the fireplace, and more, give special meaning to a Lowcountry holiday. Come on in, y'all!

Ham: The Lowcountry of many coastal states is famed for hams that have been smoked according to some secret traditional recipe. Needless to say, the hams have to be ready for the holidays, since a big Christmas ham on the table is essential. Ham biscuits are a breakfast delicacy, especially if accompanied by red-eye gravy!

Hanukkah: Menorahs, dreidels, and other traditional items, foods, and celebrations can be found in the Lowcountry. Lovely synagogues are also often open for viewing during the holidays.

Historical Holiday Reenactments: It is popular in the Lowcountry for plantations, forts, historic homes, and more to host authentic Revolution-era, Colonial, or African American Gullah festivals featuring the period dress and customs of those times. Music, games, dancing, foods, and more take you back in time to days gone by on the coast. Good choices are those at Wormsloe, Middleton Place, Drayton Hall, Fort Jackson, and many others.

Hog Killing Time: Sometime after Thanksgiving, when it finally grew cool enough, it was time for hog killing in the Lowcountry. This was usually a family and friends affair since time was of the essence. A well-fatted hog would be killed, washed, scrubbed, eviscerated, and cut down into its many parts so that all was used "but the squeal." This putting-up of the hog—corning it, smoking it, making sausage—or other preparations was important to have meat through the winter. It's also common to have "pig-pickings" even at Christmas. A hole is dug in the ground and a hog is baked on a grill over hot coals, all covered in wet burlap. This is a day-long event and ends with a delicious meal of barbecued pork, watermelon rind pickles, potato salad, hushpuppies, and most likely, banana pudding. It's even more fun if there's a chill in the air and you have to bundle up a bit over a beach bonfire.

Holiday Happenings: One thing about the Lowcountry is that even at Christmas it's usually warm enough to enjoy activities, such as shelling, kite flying, windsurfing, kayaking, and more. The marshes take on a different kind of life, birds migrate, sand blows, and the sky and sea are especially blue.

Holly Days: While there are a great number of places to shop for the holidays in the Lowcountry, one favorite is the Holly Days Bazaar at St. John's Episcopal Church in Savannah. Not only can you find handmade crafts, you can lunch on soup, pimento cheese, shrimp salad sandwiches, and yummy desserts. Powdered sugar-coated wedding cookies are my favorite!

Hurricanes: In the Lowcountry, this usually means a storm, but at Christmastime, it means lovely glass-enclosed candles often decorated with holly. Early hurricane lamps were more elaborate glass affairs. Enclosed candles were helpful in coastal breezes, but today they are mainly a source of romance and beauty on a dinner table or outdoor porch. (But just because hurricane season is over at the end of November does not mean that a tropical storm or hurricane can't hit the Lowcountry any time of the year.)

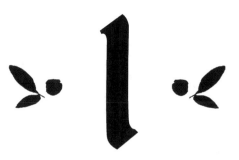

Inn the Mood!: Nothing will get you in a Lowcountry Christmas mood more than staying in one of the many lovely inns or bed and breakfasts. Just one example is the Rhett House Inn in Beaufort, a 9,000-square-foot 1820 antebellum mansion with a lovely verandah.

Jenny Lind: In Christmas 1850, the famous "Swedish Nightingale," Jenny Lind, visited Charleston, South Carolina, as part of a P.T. Barnum tour in America. The crowds were so large to hear her sing that a phrase "a squeeze equal to a Jenny Lind concert" became widely used. Although she could sing like a nightingale, Jenny was quite private. She spent Christmas Day in her Charleston Hotel room, but donated $500 to the Charleston Ladies' Benevolent Society. One high society woman who really wanted to meet the singer dressed as a maid and tried to take tea to her room, but was thwarted. Others put a tree with colorful lamps at her window to help Jenny have a Merry Christmas in the Holy City.

Jest 'fore Christmas

Father calls me William, sister calls me Will, Mother calls me Willie, but the fellers call me Bill! Mighty glad I ain't a girl — ruther be a boy, Without them sashes, curls, an'things that's worn by Fauntleroy! Love to chawnk green apples an'go swimmin' in the lake — Hate to take the castor-ile they give for belly-ache! 'Most all the time, the whole year round, there ain't no flies on me, But jest 'fore Christmas I'm good as I kin be!

Got a yeller dog named Sport, sic him on the cat; First thing she knows she doesn't know where she is at! Got a clipper sled, an'when us kids goes out to slide, 'Long comes the grocery cart, an'we all hook a ride! But sometimes when the grocery man is worried an'cross, He reaches at us with his whip, an'larrups up his hoss, An'then I laff an'holler, "Oh, ye never teched me!" But jest 'fore Christmas I'm good as I kin be!

Love Songs of Childhood, Eugene Field, 1894

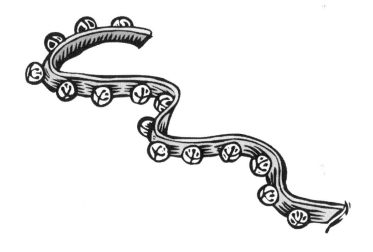

"Jingle Bells": One lesser-known Lowcountry Christmas trivia is that James L. Pierpont (1822-1893) composed this popular tune when he was the music director of a Unitarian Church in downtown Savannah. A prolific songwriter, he was also the uncle of famed financier John Pierpont Morgan. He married the daughter of the mayor of Savannah and served with a Confederate cavalry regiment. You can see a historic marker regarding "Jingle Bells" on Oglethorpe Square. What ever prompted him to write about dashing through the snow in the sunny South is unknown!

Jingle Jog Run: Christmas day runs on the beach are popular in the Lowcountry. The theme usually includes dressing as some kind of surfer Santa and wearing plenty of bells. Even doggies get into the act! Of course, later they need a nap on your new favorite Christmas throw!

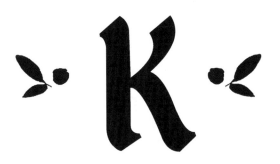

Knucklehead Christmas

Of course, Christmas comes to the Carolinas every year! But in some years, times are hard. Traditions may be interrupted by poverty or illness. Here's how one Lowcountry family celebrated a "Hard Times Christmas"…

Life was not easy for the Knuckle family. Father was away from home trying to earn money. Mother was very sick. Grandmother took care of her and the three children—who everyone called the "Knuckleheads!"

The Knuckleheads wanted to have Christmas so badly! They made stockings out of paper. They called them "Tussie Mussies." They looked like ice cream cones! They hung them by the fire on the night before Christmas.

The next morning, the Knuckleheads found their stockings full to the brim! Each Tussie Mussie held nuts, pine needles, pine cones, flower petals, holly berries, tree bark, sea shells and other goodies. It smelled wonderful! "Let's give it to mother!" they decided. Mother Knuckle was so happy. "Do you know what this is?" she asked. "It's called potpourri. It makes things smell sweet. What a beautiful gift!"

The children beamed with pride. Their Christmas gifts were next. There was a brand new baby sister in Mother's bed! Then, Father appeared in the doorway! He was home! And as he leaned over to kiss them, a couple of pine needles, *holly berries, and tree bark fell from his pocket! The children laughed with delight! Christmas Never Smelled So Sweet!*

"Koonering": "Do you remember when we used to go Koonering?" is a common preface to many North Carolina reminisces. First observed on plantations, slaves would outfit themselves in outlandish costumes and masks and appear at Christmas to sing ritual dances. Later, the practice was carried on by aristocratic city youth — primarily to impress their beaus!

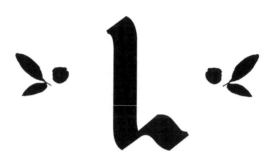

Legend of the Christmas Flower

Long ago, there lived a poor young girl in the country of Mexico. Each year, her church held a Christmas Eve service. People from miles around came to place gifts by the nativity scene for the Christ Child.

The little girl was sad because she had no gift for the baby. She sat down and wept outside the church. An angel heard her and whispered something in her ear. The little girl jumped to her feet and gathered some weeds from the side of the road. The weeds turned into beautiful poinsettias to be laid at the altar.

What did the angel say to the girl? According to the legend, he said that even a very plain gift is worth a lot if it is given with love. And ever since, the green leaves of the poinsettia turn red every Christmas as an everlasting gift!

Which state grows the most poinsettias? California!

Poinsettias are found all over the Carolinas at Christmastime. Sometimes you'll even see them stacked up in the shape of a Christmas tree!

Lowcountry Legend, Lore & Superstition

Some Carolinians believe that doing certain things at Christmastime can protect you or bring you good luck...or bad luck! Here are some of these superstitions from the past:

GOOD LUCK

Hang holly on the door at Christmastime to keep away evil spirits and protect the house from lightning.

Save a piece of charcoal from a Yule log to protect you from thunder and lightning.

Eat an apple at 12:00 on Christmas Eve to have good

health throughout the coming year.

The first person to bring holly into the house at Christmas will rule the household for the following year.

BAD LUCK

A meowing cat on Christmas is bad luck.

Do not wash and press a Christmas present before giving. It washes out the good luck and presses in the bad luck.

A man should run from redheaded women at Christmas.

Evil spirits will come to your house if you let the fire go out on Christmas.

Lowcountry Legends: There are many coastal holiday legends. One is that on Christmas Eve, the animals can talk. Another is the appearance of Old Buck, a shipwreck survivor. The wild ponies of the Outer Banks are living legends, as are the ponies of Chincoteague on the Virginia coast.

Old Buck

Musical Instruments: Drum, dulcimer, harpsichord, harmonica, banjo, guitar, piano, and even bagpipes can be part of any Lowcountry Christmas musical celebrations.

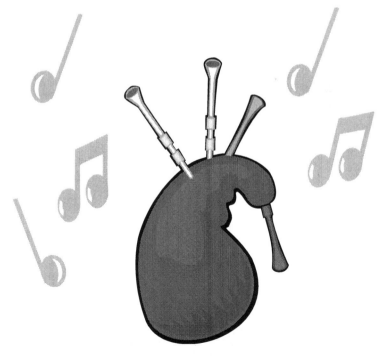

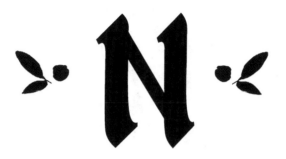

Naps: If you must settle down for a long winter's nap after your holiday feast, do it the Lowcountry way—either in a low-slung rope hammock or upon a hanging bed (that swings) on a front or back porch, preferably overlooking the Atlantic Ocean.

New Year's Day: The "essential" Lowcountry meal on January 1 was (and often is) a large baked or smoked ham, collard greens (for money in the new year), rice or Hoppin' John (for luck), and blackeyed peas for change (as in pennies, dimes, etc.). Cornbread, or better yet, cracklin' cornbread, made in a cast iron skillet, was a must-have. And red-eye gravy made from the ham grease was wonderful over the rice or hot, homemade biscuits. Collard greens are always tastiest after the first frost (lucky if happens before Christmas), when the now-wilted greens are sweet!

New Year's Eve: Firecrackers were always popular on New Year's Eve, especially in the colonial era. Today, they are just as popular, even when illegal! While almost every Lowcountry town puts on some kind of fireworks show, it's also fun to camp out on the beach or a dock and twist your head left and right to keep up with the sparkle all up and down the waterways and beyond.

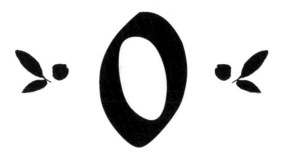

Old Buck: This ancient tradition on the Outer Banks in the small town of Rodan celebrates Old Buck, a legendary bull that supposedly survived a shipwreck dating back to the early Elizabethan era. Of course, it includes a bonfire and an oyster roast and the appearance of Old Buck, much to the delight of those Lowcountry children.

Oyster Dressing: A popular dish to go with the Christmas meal was not just dressing (what we call stuffing in the Lowcountry), but a moist cornmeal concoction filled with plump, fresh May River oysters! Roasted oysters involved a soaking wet burlap sack to steam them over the hot coals of an outdoor fire. Add chopped celery, onion, broth, and lots of fresh sage and bake until golden. Serve with turkey gravy.

Oysters: It's impossible to celebrate Christmas in the Lowcountry without oysters. Popular holiday dishes include oyster stew, oysters Rockefeller, oyster dressing, oyster casserole, and more. Oyster shells are used to make decorations like oyster angels for the Christmas tree.

Oyster Soup or Stew: A popular Christmas Eve meal, often served with chili. While my grandmother and husband made great oyster stew, I always loved that made at the Island Inn on Ocracoke. The broth was salty as the sea and the clams and oysters floated happily down my hatch!

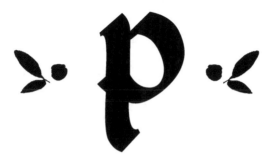

Pancakes & Presents: In the Lowcountry, it is traditional and popular to serve Christmas Brunch. You often start with Bloody Marys or Mimosas, and move on to smoked ham, eggs Benedict, cheese grits, tomato aspic, and other yummy fare like biscuits smothered in red-eye or sawmill gravy, and sweets like red velvet pancakes. Needless to say, after the gifts are opened, a nap often follows, unless you are off to the Hunt!

Parades: In addition to the traditional Christmas parades in most Lowcountry towns, there are also boat parades, usually held at dusk, on creeks and harbors, featuring craft as small as a dinghy to large yachts, Santa aboard many, some with jumping dolphin or fish.

Pirate's Christmas: Ahoy and Merry Christmas, me hearties!

Aye, aye, matey! Even Lowcountry pirates celebrated Christmas! Their annual "Saturnalia" was a big pirate party. The idea for it came from a very old religious holiday.

Pirates were good cooks, too. They often had a lot of free time when they weren't doing the things that pirates do! So they explored the closest island and used whatever local meats, fish, plants, or fruits they could find. Stew was a favorite meal!

Plantations: A great Lowcountry holiday tour is one that encompasses some of the major plantations from Charleston to Savannah. Favorites include Wormsloe, Drayton Hall, Middleton Place, Boone Hall, Williamsburg, Somerset Place, Tryon Palace, and many others. It's a great way to see costumed performers reenact Olde Christmas in the Lowcountry. Add shopping and eating and you feel like you are back in the 1800s!

Poem: Have a Carolina CHRISTMAS!

A Carolina Christmas
Is like crystallizing glass
As it hardens to tradition
Which we treasure so to last.

In the Carolina cities
Christmas's fest & feast & fun
Heaps of holly, loads of lights
And bales of hot cross buns.

In the Carolina country
Christmas sniffs of sweets'
Of cinnamon & peppermint
And rotisserie-ing meats!
On the Carolina coast
The ocean joins the celebration

By scalloping the shoreline
With white foam decoration.

Yes, Christmas in Carolina
Is eclectic to say the least
Where a popcorn & paperchain tree's equal
To a Charleston low country feast!

Harmonica & harpsichord
Both are equal to praise the Lord.

So's a supper of oyster stew
And syllabub and chess pie, too!

Cornucopias dangle from city trees
Country halls with gingham bedeck

While a seahorse on an island pine
Boasts a bow around his neck!
Christmas in Carolina's magnolia &
Queen Anne's lace,

A "Catfish Stomp" in Elgin
The shag, and hounds giving chase.

And those Carolina kids & grandkids!
We know they're the sweetest bar none
At least from the first of December
'Til Christmas Day around one!

And after a Carolina Christmas
You can return anything you please
There's only one exception
All those calories!

—Carole Marsh Longmeyer

Poinsettia: This Christmas plant was named for a Charlestonian, botanist, physician, and politician—Joel Roberts Poinsett. He discovered the shrub while serving as the first U.S. Ambassador to Mexico in the 1820s. He brought cuttings back to his South Carolina greenhouse and later shared plants with friends and fellow gardeners. A story tagged along with the plant that an angel came to a girl who did not have a gift for the Christ child's birthday. The angel told her to gather weeds and put them at the church altar. Red blossoms sprouted to create a Christmas legend. Today, hybrid plants come in white, peppermint-like red and white, and even a red and white spackle pattern. For five generations, the Oelschig Nursery in Savannah has grown more than 40,000 plants in its 120,000 square foot greenhouse to bloom in time for the holidays.

Polar Bear Plunge: One of the most popular of these brave, but crazy, events is held on the beach at Tybee

Island, Georgia, each year. Chilly water is not so bad if followed by a bowl of hot crab stew!

Pomanders: This old-fashioned colonial gift made the house or cabin smell good. A large orange was stuck with cloves and then attached to a ribbon so it could be hung.

Potpourri Recipe: Outdoors, collect nuts, berries, pine needles and cones, cedar tree bark, and other natural materials. Add flower petals; roses are especially good; it's ok if they are dead and dried up. From the kitchen, add rosemary, thyme, parsley, or other herbs and spices. Other things you might add include: cotton balls, moss, baby's breath from old flower arrangements, dried peas and beans, bits of ribbon, lace, or colored paper, crayon, soap, or pencil shavings, slivers of orange rind, white or wild rice, etc. Sprinkle your potpourri mixture with a few drops of perfume, baby powder, or cinnamon. Stir well. Use to fill your Tussie Mussie.

Puddings: In the colonial-era in the Lowcountry, puddings were pretty much the queens of the holiday table. Age-old recipes were often combined with new-found ingredients in the New World. Puddings included steamed cranberry with honey sauce, steamed plum pudding, steamed pumpkin pudding with rum sauce, old-fashioned suet pudding, baked Indian pudding, steamed persimmon pudding with hard sauce, and walnut soufflé with lemon sauce. But the most favored was tasty Eight Treasures Rice Pudding.

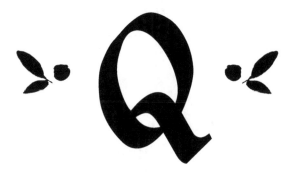

Quarters: In the slave quarters, slaves had a custom called "Christmas Gif." Children tried to see someone else before they were seen. The first one to call out "Christmas Gif" was the winner. The loser had to give a gift of a few nuts or a cupcake. The tradition spread from the slave quarters to the master's house. "Christmas Gif" became a tradition in the Old South. Slaves in the Lowcountry would also find a big green tree at the end of each Christmas season. They cut it down and put it in the swamp. Then they brought it to the plantation the next Christmas. The holiday season lasted until the Yule Log burned in two. Many slaves did not have to work as long as the log burned!

Quilts: From early American history, the quilt was a part of winter, indeed, a necessity. The Lowcountry gets cold, too, and historical quilts made by African slaves or early colonists are collector's items today. Quilting bees still exist, though in fewer numbers. Museums love to host quilt exhibits. A true Lowcountry quilt might just as likely feature crabs and fish as traditional motifs. Holiday gift bazaars often have a raffle of a holiday quilt which may end up as a family keepsake hauled out of the attic each year for the holidays.

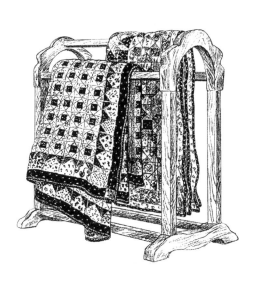

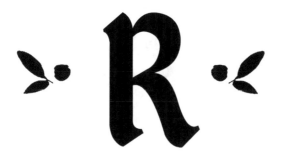

Rural decorations: It is common in the Lowcountry to slap colored lights on everything from lighthouses to live oaks. A drive down Lowcountry roads in December can bring to light delights such as bulb-festooned tractors, fences, farm houses, coastal cottages, and almost anything else, all very pretty.

One of our favorite things (my husband and I) was to take any winter trip that invoved driving down coastal (or near-coastal) roads in the dead of winter, just before Christmas. We have spied lighthouses adorned with wreaths or colored lights. Coastal towns might string lights across the streets, which is a very old-fashioned look. It just makes a happy time to travel!

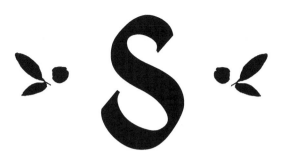

Salmagundi Stew: In a large cooking pot, put cut-up chunks of chicken, roast pork, beef, ham, and fish. Cover with broth and simmer until well done and tender. (Pirates added pigeon and other birds.) Add chopped cabbage, chopped hardboiled eggs, chopped onions, carrots, and any other vegetables you enjoy. (Pirates also added anchovies, olives, and grapes.) Cover with more broth and simmer until vegetables are tender. Add spices, such as garlic, salt, pepper, mustard seed, or other. (Pirates sometimes added gunpowder!) Serve hot in bowls with hardtack (or hard rolls), and a fruit salad with poppyseed dressing. (Yes, pirates ate salad!) Avast!

Shiver me timbers! Did ye know that the word "barbecue" comes from "buccaneer," which means "cookers of meat"?!

Yo-ho-ho! Would ye have ever guessed that Blackbeard—the Carolinas' best-known buccaneer—has been known to appear on Christmas cards?!

Santa Claus: The jolly old elf can be seen all around the Lowcountry during the Christmas season. A lot of towns have Jolly Trolleys with Santa aboard and carols sung.

Secret Pocket
Christmas Quilt

Even in colonial Carolina days, Christmas was about secrets and surprises. Once upon a time, from Thanksgiving to December, women hunkered down by oil lamp or firelight to make Christmas gifts. One popular gift for those cold winter nights was a fluffy, new quilt! Quilts were often made from patchwork, patches of fabric from old dresses, seed sacks, and even men's ties. These colorful, mismatched scraps were sewn into beautiful quilts stuffed with cotton or even straw. The patterns included log cabins, flowers, or other designs. Sometimes the quilts told a story... if you knew how to translate the hidden message. Slaves once gave directions for safe travel along the Underground Railroad. But the Christmas quilt might also include a special surprise—a secret pocket! One quilt square would be left with an unfinished edge, creating a small "pocket." Into this holiday hiding place, a mother might tuck a special gift like a ring, necklace, toy, or candy.

Shipwrecks and Stories

You never know what might start a Christmas tradition! Rodanthe, North Carolina, has two traditions based on mysterious shipwrecks!

Once upon a time...a Scottish boy named Donald McDonald survived a shipwreck by holding tight to his floating drum. He was rescued from the angry sea on Hatteras Island. His drum survives to this day! Folks in Rodanthe believe it has magical qualities.

The town of Rodanthe celebrates Old Christmas on January 6. The day is filled with good food and great games. But in the evening it happens! Donald's drum is heard and Old Buck the bull appears! The children are frightened, but they must scare Old Buck away. He charges through the crowd and back out into the darkness. The brave children of Rodanthe have saved Christmas once more!

If you must know, Old Buck is really two boys hiding under a cowhide!

How did Old Buck get here? Another shipwreck at Wimble

Shoals killed a load of cattle coming to the New World. Only one bull survived. Legend says he ran off into the thick, green woods. Residents called him Old Buck, and say that he's still there!

Slave Quarters at Christmas: During the era of slavery in the South, even the slaves were allowed to celebrate the holidays. One special celebration took place in the Lowcountry rice plantation of Somerset Place.

Sleigh Rides: While we don't have sleigh rides in the Lowcountry, there are plenty of winter hay rides in farm wagons pulled by horses or mules, Christmas golf cart parades, boat parades from rowboats to yachts, and dune buggies to pull boogie boarders down the beach!

Snow: We seldom have snow in the Lowcountry, but when we do it is a real treat (and often, a real mess!). I have seen the Pamlico River on the North Carolina coast freeze over and stop the state ferry system from running—something almost unheard of. Snow on the beach seems like a miracle and is very pretty. If Lowcountry kids draw pictures of snow, it always has brown sticks sticking up—that's the grass! So we make do with pine cones—have plenty of those in the piney woods—and red and green snow cones!

Stockings Were Hung: A whimsical variety of Christmas stockings can be found in historical Lowcountry homes and manses. Long, thin red-and-white-striped stockings…lovely, lacy Victorian almost shoe-like stockings…long white fisherman's socks…and many more.

Stringing popcorn: In colonial days, it was popular for children to popcorn over an open fire, then string it to make garland for the tree. The more they snacked, the shorter the garland!

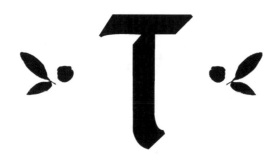

Take Me to Church: Whether small, white rural AME churches or enormous cathedrals in Savannah or Charleston, all Lowcountry church buildings are beautifully decorated at Christmastime. My own Trinity United Methodist Church (1848) adorns its large wooden doors with live wreaths. Inside, the sanctuary is festooned with pine swags and red ribbon, a Chrismon tree, and poinsettias. Lowcountry churches often offer holiday tours, and always are open to members, guests, and visitors from near and far.

Terrapin Stew: One Lowcountry holiday delicacy was once exported to places like New York City and Russia—terrapins for turtle soup, popular on Christmas Eve, as is oyster stew.

Ticket Booth Cottage: This quaint structure on Tybee Island is a one-room guest cottage that was once a part of the railroad that brought visitors from Savannah. Today it's popular on Christmas tours, as are other cottages, such as Little Palm, Mermaid, and Amazing Grace, in this quaint Georgia beach town.

Toys: In the old days, the standard cornhusk dolls, wooden trains, teddy bears, and more, were popular beneath the tree. Today, Lowcountry kids pine for a new surf- or boogie-board, swim fins, snorkeling gear, fishing rod, beach bike, or other water-related play equipment, like the Christmas parade popular giant squirt guns!

Tussie-Mussies: A simple Lowcountry decoration was this old-English paper cone filled with potpourri, peppermints, small toys, gingerbread cookies, or other items. The paper cones were decorated with lace, ribbon, or other items and tucked into the Christmas tree branches.

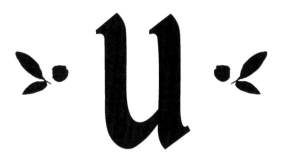

Under the Mistletoe: A popular pastime in the Lowcountry is shooting mistletoe, such as red-beribboned kissing balls, out of trees for holiday decorating. If you think you have never seen mistletoe growing naturally, look again. In December, high up in leafless oak trees, you will spot these perfectly round balls of green. Some are small, others quite large.

Mistletoe may seem romantic, but it's actually a parasite. In fact the name comes from 'mistel" and "tan," which sort of means poop on a stick! It is poisonous to humans, but not to bees that could create Christmas honey from the pollen it collects from the plant.

Victorian Lowcountry Christmas:
Victorian houses were often decorated with "gingerbread"— fancy, cut-out pieces of wooden trim. When we imagine "picture book" or "fairytale" type Christmases in our mind...what we often picture is Christmas in Savannah or Charleston in the Victorian Era! The

Victorians were the first to go all-out with Christmas trees, stockings hung by the chimney with care, gifts and goodies, caroling, and decorations. A widow's walk was a balcony on top of the roof, where the wife would go to watch and see if her husband was coming home from the sea or the war. Victorian children dressed like little adults. Girls wore bloomers, petticoats, long, fancy dresses, and lace-up boots. Boys wore stiff shirts, ascots (scarf ties), waistcoats (vests), long jackets, and lace-up boots. In the Victorian Era, people decorated with natural materials, such as fresh pine boughs and red holly berries. Imagine little girls and boys dressed in fancy clothes, with ringlets in their hair, sitting on overstuffed sofas by a roaring fire waiting for Santa to come. Victorian Christmases were sometimes celebrated with elaborate parties with music, dancing, and pastries piled high. The children might make pull taffy and play a Cobweb party game where they snarled a room with yarn. To play, each child ducked in and out of the "cobweb" to find a Christmas toy at the end of their colored string. Victorians put potpourri under their pillows to have "sweet dreams."

Village Life: One holiday event not to miss is the annual Gingerbread Village competition held at the Westin Savannah Harbor. At the fundraiser, you'll see gingerbread houses, churches, bridges, lighthouses, and more—all local sites—built and decorated by children to professionals. The highlight is a chef-created Westin itself in gingerbread glory. It's all pretty impressive and part of the Thanksgiving-to-New Year's community celebration.

Wassailing: This merry old English tradition waded its way to the New World. Lowcountry Christmas soirees in the grand mansions along the Battery in Charleston, in the drawing rooms on the Virginia coast, and in the antebellum homes of Savannah are certain to serve spiced tea, eggnog, cranberry-orange punch, spiced cider, Artillery Punch, and other concoctions during the holidays. In a cut-glass antique punch bowl, heaped with homemade whipped cream, and most likely, spiked with one or more kinds of liquor, the celebrations begin!

Wine: Popular Lowcountry wines to serve with Christmas dinner include dandelion wine, plum wine, scuppernong wine, and others. Over the last few years, wineries have popped up everywhere in the Lowcountry, adding new flavors to the holiday.

Wreaths: Lowcountry wreaths adorn everything from lighthouses to front doors, gates and garrisons, bows of sailboats and stalls in horse barns. Made of whatever greenery is available, they are often decorated with pine cones, holly berries, lemons, pineapples, apples, peacock feathers, seashells, sand dollars, and any other available natural items. Most are "bowed" with velvet, nautical rope, calico ribbons, burlap bows, or garden twine.

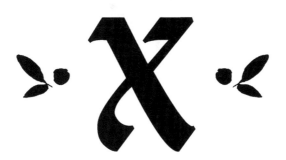

Xtinguisher: Lacking the protection of a horse-drawn fire wagon or a pressurized water system, Lowcountry folks often devised their own homemade fire extinguishers from common household substances. One part baking soda mixed with three parts fine sand yielded an adequate powder extinguisher. Stored in bottles or tins at strategic locations throughout the home, the inexpensive concoction could be thrown at the base of the flames in the event of a flare-up.

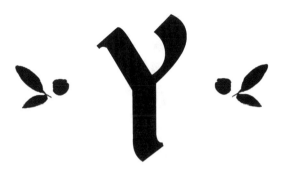

Yule Log: Don't miss the many living history demonstrations during the holidays in the Lowcountry. The lighting of the yule log, blacksmithing, tabby-making, and more abound at various locations. Magazines like *Southern Living*, *Garden and Gun*, *Coastal Living*, and others begin to advertise such events in early November.

Zing the Carols: Popular in colonial America until the present, ancient carols are still sung in churches, while informal holiday songs may be sung door-to-door in Lowcountry neighborhoods or around a beach bonfire.

LOWCOUNTRY CHRISTMAS
Receipts

"Receipts" is an old-fashioned term for recipes.

Tomato Aspic •✔

A refreshing, old-fashioned holiday dish, this looks very Christmasy since it's red and topped with sour cream and parsley. In a bowl, sprinkle 2 tablespoons of unflavored gelatin (get a box in the grocery store baking section) over 1/2 cup of cold water and let soak for 3 minutes. In a saucepan, mix 3 and 1/2 cups of tomato juice, gelatin, 2 tablespoons onion juice, 1 and 2/3 tablespoons lemon juice, 1 teaspoon sugar, and 3/4 tablespoon Worcestershire sauce. Bring to a boil and stir until gelatin dissolves. Let simmer 15 minutes. Add 1 cup of finely chopped green olives (with pimento centers), 1 cup finely chopped celery, and 1 cup of finely chopped pecans. Pour into a pretty mold; a bundt cake pan will do nicely. Let chill at least five hours. To unmold, carefully hold mold into lukewarm water until you feel the aspic begin to give way a bit. Place a plate or platter larger than the mold over the mold, and quickly turn it over. If you are lucky, the aspic will slip to the platter in one piece! Surround with butter lettuce. Top with a dollop of sour cream and parsley.

Waldorf Salad

In a large bowl, combine a couple of crisp, sweet apples that have been cored and chopped into nickel- or dime-sized pieces. Add 1 cup of celery, thinly sliced, 1 cup of chopped, slightly toasted walnuts, 2 bananas peeled and sliced thin (not too ripe!), a dozen maraschino cherries, stemmed and cut in half, at least 6 tablespoons of mayonnaise and two heaping tablespoons of whipped cream. Mix all gently but thoroughly. Chill and serve over baby lettuce leaves. This was a popular Lowcountry holiday dish.

Saltwater Taffy

This version of old-fashioned pull taffy was, and still is, a fun activity for children of all ages.

2 c. brown sugar
4 T. molasses
2 t. butter
1/3 c. water
1 T. vinegar
pinch of baking soda

In a heavy saucepan, cook brown sugar until it dissolves. Add remaining ingredients and cook (stir occasionally) until mixture reaches hard-ball stage. Pour into a buttered pan and let cool. When still warm, rub butter on your hands and pull the taffy back and forth until it has a satiny finish. Cut with scissors into small pieces and wrap in wax paper, twisting the ends.

Spiced Tea •🌿

1 gallon boiling water, 6 tea balls, 1 and 1/2 c. sugar, 1 t. cinnamon, 1 t. cloves, 6 oranges, 4 lemons, 1 quart grape juice. Add rum as desired.

Steep tea balls in boiling water for 10 minutes. Remove tea balls. Add sugar, cinnamon, cloves, and the juice of the oranges and lemons. Add grape juice; bring to a boil. Add rum, if wish, to taste. Serve warm.

Eggnog •🌿

This was the punch bowl drink of choice for Lowcountry holidays.

4 eggs, well beaten
1/3 c. sugar
1/2 t. nutmeg
4 T. lemon juice

1/8 t. salt
4 c. whole milk
1/2 c. thick cream
rum
homemade whipped cream

Into beaten eggs, blend sugar, nutmeg, lemon juice, and salt. Add milk and cream. Beat mixture until frothy. Add rum to taste, if desired. Chill well. Serve in a large punch bowl. Add dollops of homemade whipped cream.

Eight Treasures Rice Pudding

1 8 oz. pkg. dates
1/2 c. water
1 c. sugar
10 almonds, blanched
1/3 c. raisins
1 c. dried apricots, chopped
5 T. lard

1/2 c. cashew nuts
1/2 c. pineapple chunks, drained
12 maraschino cherries
4 c. cooked rice
pinch of salt
Rich Warm Sauce (see below for recipe)

Finely chop all dates except 12. Mix dates with water, 1/4 cup sugar, and 2 T. lard. Combine and cook; stir until thickened. In the bottom of a greased mold arrange the rest of the fruits and nuts. Mix rice, remaining sugar and lard and pack half into the fruit-lined mold. Spoon in the thickened date mixture and top with remaining rice. Steam for 1/2 hour. Unmold and serve with Rich Warm Sauce.

Rich Warm Sauce

1 T cornstarch
1/4 c. sugar

1 c. water
1/2 c. cherry juice

Blend cornstarch and sugar into water and juice. Cook over medium heat until thick and clear. Serve hot over the Eight Treasures Rice Pudding.

Gullah-Geechee Gingerbread

2 fresh eggs
1/4 c. brown sugar
1/4 c. real molasses
1/4 c. melted butter
2 1/2 c. flour
2 t. ginger
1 1/2 t. cinnamon
1/2 t. cloves
1/2 t. nutmeg
1/2 t. baking powder
1 c. boiling water
peaches

Preheat oven to 350 degrees. Beat eggs and add to sugar, molasses, and melted butter. Sift the dry ingredients and add to liquid mixture. Add boiling water last. Bake in shallow pain for approximately 30 minutes. Serve warm with peaches.

Old Slave Molasses Pie

1 c. sugar
1 T. butter softened
2 c. molasses
3 fresh eggs
Juice of fresh lemon
ground nutmeg
1 unbaked 9-inch pie shell

Combine ingredients. Pour mixture into pie shell and bake at 350 degrees until set and crust is brown.

According to superstition, you should save the pointed tip of a wedge of pie for the last bite.

A wish will come true if the top of the pie is cut off, pushed to the side of the plate and eaten last. Also, the wish must be repeated silently just before the last bite is taken and not a word spoken until everyone has left the dining table.

Plantation Ginger Cookies

1 c. dry bread crumbs

1/2 c. brown sugar

1/8 t. salt

1 t. ginger

1/2 t. baking soda

2 eggs, beaten

1 t. butter, melted

1 t. pure vanilla

1/4 c. molasses

Preheat oven to 400 degrees. Combine dry ingredients, then add beaten eggs, vanilla, butter, and molasses. From a spoon, drop the cookies about 2 inches apart onto a buttered baking pan. Bake for 15 minutes.

Bourbon Sweet Potatoes ❧

4 lb sweet potatoes
1/2 c. pure butter
1/4 c. fine bourbon
1/3 c. fresh orange juice
1/4 c. slightly browned sugar
1 t. salt
1/2 t. cinnamon and nutmeg, mixed
1/3 c. chopped pecans

Preheat oven to 350 degrees. Cook and mash the sweet potatoes. Add butter, bourbon, orange juice, salt and spices. Beat well. Put mixture into buttered pan. Sprinkle with pecans and brown sugar. Bake for about 45 minutes.

Enterprise Peanut Brittle ❧

1 c. sugar
1/2 c. white Karo syrup
1/4 c. hot water

1 t. butter
2 c. raw peanuts
1 t. pure vanilla
1 t. baking soda

Bring syrup, sugar and water to a boil. Add butter and peanuts. Boil and stir constantly until the peanuts start to pop and syrup starts to brown. Remove from the heat and add vanilla and baking soda. Work very fast. Pour on a greased marble slab, smooth out, and let cool. Break into chunks and serve or store.

Women in the South had to fight for survival during and after the Civil War. Sugar became scarce, so sorghum became the standard sweetener. The women learned to make a substitute for ordinary baking soda from the ashes of corn cobs. These ashes were placed in a jar and covered with water to stand until clear. By using one part ashes and two parts sour milk, various sweet items could be made.

Cheese Straws

1 stick pure butter
2 c. sharp cheese, grated
1 t. baking powder
1/2 t. salt
1 1/2 c. sifted flour
1/4 t. cayenne

Preheat oven to 400 degrees. Cream butter well. Add cheese and blend. Stir in dry ingredients. Roll out the mixture to a thickness of about 1/2 inch and cut into strips about 1/2 inch wide. Bake for 25 minutes or until done.

Sugared Pecans

Mix 1/2 cup sugar and 1/2 cup water and boil until the syrup spins a thread. Continue cooking until the mixture reaches a soft ball stage. Remove from the heat. Add some grated orange rind and stir until foamy. Stir in 1 pound shelled pecans, carefully coating each one well. Pour into a lightly greased dish and separate with the tines of a fork while the syrup is still warm. Let the pecans harden and cool.

Divinity

2 c. pure maple syrup
1/4 t. salt
egg whites
1/2 c. unbroken pecans

Butter the sides of a heavy saucepan and cook the syrup rapidly over a high heat to the hard ball stage (250 degrees on a candy thermometer) without stirring. Remove from heat. All at once, add the salt to the egg whites and beat to very stiff peaks. Pour the hot syrup slowly over the stiff egg whites, beating constantly and as fast as you can. Beat until the mixture forms soft peaks and begins to lose its gloss. Add the nuts and drop by teaspoons onto a buttered pan.

Bluffton Eggnog Pound Cake

1 c. butter
1 c. shortening
3 c. sugar
6 eggs
3 c. all-purpose flour
1 c. eggnog
1 c. flaked coconut
1 t. lemon extract
1 t. vanilla extract
1 t. coconut extract
whipped cream for garnish
nutmeg for garnish

Preheat oven to 325 degrees. Cream together butter and shortening. Gradually add sugar, beating well. Add eggs one at a time, beating well after each addition. Using a spoon, add flour to creamed mixture alternating with the eggnog. Stir in coconut and flavorings. Blend well.

Pour batter into a well-greased and floured 10-inch pan. Bake at 325 degrees for 1 1/2 hours. Remove from oven and allow to cool for 10 minutes before removing cake from pan. Top with whipped cream and sprinkle with grated nutmeg.

Hot Holiday Punch

1 gallon cranapple juice
1 liter lemon/lime soda
1/2 gallon white grape juice
1/4 c. lime juice
2 oz. cinnamon sticks
cheesecloth
1/2 T. cloves

2 c. brandy (optional)

Put liquid ingredients in a large kettle and place on top of stove. Wrap cinnamon sticks and cloves in cheesecloth and place in the pot. Simmer for 45 minutes over medium heat and remove. Pour punch into a serving bowl and ladle into punch cups.

Epiphany Surprise Christmas Cake ✥

Many people still celebrate "Old Christmas" by baking an Epiphany Cake. Families enjoy making old-fashioned *puuuuuuuul* taffy! And our beautiful churches inspired stained-glass window cookies!

Bake any boxed cake mix according to the directions on the package. For a little extra holiday flavor, add

1 teaspoon peppermint extract. Just before you put the cake into the oven to bake, drop in the following items: 1 black-eyed pea, 1 large lima bean, 1 large button, 1 dime, 1 thimble, 1 ring, 1 heart, and 1 whole clove. After the cake is baked, you can frost it, if you wish. You can also add 1 teasoon peppermint flavoring to the frosting. **When the cake is served, remind everyone to be very careful—to find their surprise with their fork first, before biting into the cake.**

Once everyone has their surprise, you can tell them what each item means:

pea = power
bean = wisdom
button = faith
dime = wealth
thimble = patience
ring = friendship
heart = love
clove = foolishness

Old-Fashioned Pull Taffy •⦗

2 1/2 c. sugar
1/2 c. water
1/4 c. vinegar
1/8 t. salt
1 T. margarine
1 t. peppermint extract

Combine the first 5 ingredients in large pot. Cook, without stirring, over medium heat just until mixture reaches the soft crack stage (270 degrees). Remove from heat; stir in peppermint. Pour candy onto a well-buttered cookie sheet. Let cool; *puuuuuul* candy until it grows light in color and becomes difficult to *puuuuuuul.* (Butter your hands if the candy is too sticky.) Divide the candy in half and pull into a rope, 1 inch in diameter. Cut the taffy into 1-inch pieces; wrap each piece in waxed paper. Makes about 40 pieces. Clean up kitchen. Wash hands. Taste taffy. Yuuuuuum!

Stained Glass Cookies •ᐸ

Pre-made sugar cookie dough (keep refrigerated until use)

1 bag sour-ball candies or 3 packs of Life Savers (assorted colors)

Preheat oven to 350 degrees. Line two baking sheets with aluminum foil. Roll out pre-made cookie dough on a lightly floured surface. Use cookie cutters to make shapes from the dough. Then cut a tiny shape (like a circle, heart, or lines) in the center of each cookie. Don't cut too close to the edge, or cookies will break. Collect scraps of dough, roll it again, and cut more shapes until all the dough is used. Make sure dough stays cold. Separate the candies by color and fill a plastic bag with each group. Wrap one bag in a dish towel and crush the candies with a hammer. Repeat process with each bag. Candies should be 1/4-inch pieces or smaller. Fill the cookies with the pieces. Carefully place cookies on the baking sheets. Bake for 10-12 minutes. Cool for 10 minutes until candy hardens. Then peel cookies from foil. Store in an airtight container.

"Sandlapper" Cookies

Make a batch of sugar cookies; the frozen kind are just fine. Before baking, cut out shapes such as sea stars, seashells, and "footprints" with cookie cutters. While the cookies are still warm from baking, sprinkle sugar on them to sparkle like sand. Decorate the cookies with tube frosting to create holiday treats.

Ocracoke Clam Chowder

1 (1-inch thick) sliced salt pork
2 1/2 lb. potatoes, peeled and diced
1 1/2 pints fresh minced clams

1 onion, chopped
3 quarts water
2 1/4 t. salt

Fry salt pork over medium heat in a large Dutch oven until done. Add other ingredients and bring to a boil. Reduce heat; cover and simmer 2 hours and 15 minutes or until potatoes are tender. Yield: 8 to 12 servings.

Oyster Soup

Three pints of large fresh oysters. Two tablespoons of butter, rolled in flour. A bunch of sweet herbs. A quart of rich milk. Pepper to your taste. Take the liquor of three pints of oysters. Strain it and sit it on the fire. Put into it, pepper to your taste, two tablespoonfuls of butter rolled in flour, and a bunch of sweet marjoram and other pot herbs. When it boils, add a quart of rich milk — and as soon as it boils again, take out the herbs and put in the oysters just before you send it to the table.

— *The Cook's Own Book,* 1833

Poached Pears with Raspberry Sauce

Peel 6 firm ripe pears, leaving stems. Cut thin slice off bottom of each so it will stand upright. Place pears in large saucepan; add 4 cups cold water and 1/4 cup lemon juice. Bring to boiling; reduce heat and simmer, covered, 10 to 15 minutes. Drain. Place in baking dish; cover. Chill 3 hours or overnight. Place pears in serving dishes; pour Raspberry Sauce over pears. Makes 6 servings.

Raspberry Sauce: In blender container place 1 cup fresh or frozen unsweetened raspberries, 1/2 cup fresh orange juice,

2 tablespoons fresh lime juice, and 1/3 cup sifted powdered sugar. Blend on high speed for 1 minute. Strain to remove seeds.

Rumtoff

1 pint of fresh sweet cherries, pitted

7 c. sugar

peel of 1 orange, cut in a spiral

1 tablespoon whole cloves

1 cinnamon stick

1 t. whole allspice

1 bottle rum, brandy, or bourbon

1 pint fresh peach halves, peeled & pitted

1 pint apricot halves, peeled & pitted

1 pint plum halves, peeled & pitted

1 pint seeded or seedless grapes

1 pint fresh pineapple chunks

1 pint fresh raspberries

1 pint fresh strawberries

Scald a 6-quart stone crock with boiling water and dry it. Put cherries in it with 1 cup sugar. Add orange peel, spices, and rum. Cover crock. Add other fruits, each with a cup of sugar, stirring well after each addition. You may need to add more rum, brandy, or bourbon if the fruit has absorbed original amount. Leave crock in a dark place to ripen for 2 or 3 months.

Serve as a dessert on its own, as a sauce over ice cream, or with pound cake.

Golden Coconut Fruit Cake

1 c. sweet butter
1 1/4 c. sugar
6 eggs
2 c. flour
1 1/4 t. powdered cloves
1 1/2 t. each nutmeg and mace

2 t. cinnamon

1/2 c. sherry

1/4 c. rose water

1/2 lb each raisins, currants and coarsely chopped figs

1/2 lb citron, chopped

1 lb almonds, chopped

2 1/2 c. grated unsweetened coconut

Cream butter and sugar together until light and fluffy. Add eggs, one at a time, beating well between additions. Reserve a little flour to dredge fruits. Sift remaining flour with spices. Gradually add combined sherry and rose water and flour alternately to the butter mixture, beating well between additions. Fold in floured fruits, almonds and coconut. Turn into two 8-inch loaf pans that are buttered and lined with buttered brown paper. Bake in preheated 275-degree oven for about 3 1/2 hours, or until a tester comes out clean. Remove cakes, peel off paper, cool on a rack, wrap in foil or waxed paper and store in airtight containers. Makes about 6 pounds of cake. If you cannot get unsweetened coconut, use the sweetened type and only half the amount of sugar.

Pecan Bourbon Balls

1 c. confectioners' sugar

2 T. cocoa

2 1/2 c. crushed vanilla wafers

1 T. grated orange rind (optional)

1 1/2 c. chopped pecans

2 T. light corn syrup

1/4 c. bourbon

granulated sugar

Sift sugar and cocoa and combine with wafers, orange rind, and 1 cup nuts. Toss well to blend ingredients. Add corn syrup and bourbon and mix thoroughly. Shape into small balls, about 1 inch diameter. Roll in granulated sugar and remaining nuts. Makes about 2 dozen balls.

A Marlborough Pudding

6 pippin apples
6 T. sugar
1/4 lb butter
2 milk biscuits
1 large lemon
6 eggs
rose water
grated nutmeg
puff paste
white sugar
citron

Pare, core, and quarter six large ripe pippin apples. Stew them in about a gill of water. When they are soft but not broken, take them out, drain them through a sieve, and mash them to a paste with the back of a spoon. Mix them with six large tablespoonfuls of sugar and a quarter of a pound of butter, and set them away to get cold.

Grate two milk biscuits (or small sponge cakes or an equal quantity of stale bread) and grate the yellow peel and squeeze the juice of a large lemon. Beat six eggs light, and when the apple mixture is cold, stir them gradually into it, adding the grated biscuit and the lemon. Stir in a wine glass of rose water and a grated nutmeg.

Put the mixture into a buttered dish or dishes; lay round the edge a border of puff paste, and bake it three quarters of an hour. When cold, grate white sugar over the top, and ornament it with slips of citron handsomely arranged.

— *Directions for Cookery*, 1837

Regal Plum Pudding ✦

3 slices bread, torn into pieces
1/3-ounce can evaporated milk
2 ounces beef suet, ground
3/4 c. packed brown sugar
1 beaten egg
1/4 c. orange juice
1/2 t. vanilla
1 1/2 c. raisins
3/4 c. snipped pitted dates
1/2 c. diced mixed candied fruits and peels
1/3 c. chopped walnuts
3/4 c. all-purpose flour
1 1/2 t. ground cinnamon
3/4 t. baking soda
3/4 t. ground cloves
3/4 t. ground mace
1/4 t. salt

In a large bowl, soak torn bread in evaporated milk about 3 minutes or till softened; beat lightly to break up. Stir in suet, brown sugar, egg, orange juice, and vanilla. Add raisins, dates, candied fruits and peels, and nuts. Stir together flour, cinnamon, soda, cloves, mace, and salt. Add to fruit mixture; stir till combined. Turn mixture into a well-greased 6 1/2-cup tower mold.

Cover with foil pressed tightly against rim of the mold. Place on a rack in a deep kettle; add 1 inch of boiling water. Cover kettle; boil gently (bubbles break surface) and steam 4 hours or till done. Add more boiling water, if necessary. Cool 10 minutes before unmolding. Serve warm with Basic Hard Sauce. Makes 8 to 10 servings.

Christmas Cheer

2 750-ml bottles claret, chilled

3/4 c. sugar

1/2 t. ground nutmeg

3 7-ounce bottles carbonated water, chilled

In a punch bowl, combine the claret, sugar, and nutmeg, stirring gently till the sugar dissolves. Slowly pour in the carbonated water. Makes about 15 1/2-cup servings.

Sassafras Bark Tea

4 pieces sassafras bark (4 by 2 inches)
5 c. boiling water
5 t. sugar
cream

Place the pieces of the rosy outer bark of sassafras root in enamelware pan or teapot. Pour boiling water over bark, cover container. Let steep in a warm place for 5 minutes or until it is colored nicely. Strain into cups or into a hot teapot. Add cream and serve with sugar to make "saloop," or sweeten with honey. Serves 5.

Charleston Ice Cream Eggnog ⋅✍

12 eggs, separated
1 c. sugar
1 c. rye or bourbon whiskey
1/2 c. brandy
2 c. heavy cream, whipped
1 c. light cream
1 quart vanilla ice cream
ice

Beat egg yolks with 1/2 cup sugar until thick and very pale yellow. Gradually stir in the whiskey and brandy, stirring well. Fold in the whipped cream, gently stir in the light cream and finally fold in egg whites that have been stiffly beaten with balance of sugar. Just before serving, cut ice cream into pieces small enough to be ladled into punch cups and add to well-chilled punch bowl set in bed of ice. Makes about 18 to 20 servings.

Plantation Eggnog

12 eggs, separated
1 c. sugar
2 c. rye or bourbon whiskey
1 c. Jamaican rum
4 c. half-and-half (milk and cream)
1 c. heavy sweet cream, whipped
Powdered nutmeg

Beat yolks with 1/2 cup sugar until thick and very pale yellow. Beat in whiskey, rum, and half-and-half. In another bowl, beat egg whites, and as they begin to stiffen, gradually add remaining 1/2 cup sugar, beating well between additions. When whites are stiffly beaten, add to yolk mixture along with whipped cream. Fold together gently but thoroughly, using a rubber spatula. Serve from well-chilled punch bowl set in ice. Sprinkle with nutmeg. Makes about 18 to 20 servings.

Ham Tradition •❮

To remove the mold from an uncooked, pepper-coated ham, scrub meat with a stiff brush under hot water. Then soak ham in cold water 12 to 48 hours; change water several times. The longer the soaking, the milder the flavor. To cook, place ham, skin side up, in a large kettle. Cover with water. Simmer 20 minutes per pound or until a meat thermometer registers 160 degrees. Do not boil. Remove skin. Place ham, fat side up, on rack in a roasting pan. If desired, score ham and glaze with brown sugar or brown sugar and bread crumbs. Bake in a 400-degree oven for 15 to 20 minutes. Serve hot or cold.

Bibliography

A Farm Country Christmas: A Treasure of Heartwarming Holiday Memories
Amy Rost-Holtz, Editor

Christmas All Through the South: Joyful Memories, Timeless Moments, Enduring Traditions
A *Southern Living* Book
Forward by Rick Bragg

Christmas at Historic Houses
Patricia Hart McMillan and Katherine Kaye McMillan

A Savannah Christmas: Interiors and Traditions from the Lowcountry
Kimberly Ergul and Holley Jaakkola

Merry
Lowcountry
Christmas,
Y'all!

About the Author

Carole Marsh Longmeyer lives for Christmas in the Lowcountry! As an author, she has visited many coastal historic sites during the holidays. "Any historic site is twice as good with cocoa and peppermint!" She has autographed books at the historic Biltmore House and many other Lowcountry locales. "I have even seen snow on Ocracoke Island at Christmas!" she says. "Oysters taste better grilled over a yule log bonfire, and Plantation eggnog tastes wonderful year round!" Every December, I get my jingle jog on! Hope you do, too!"

About the Designer

Susan Van Denhende is a freelance illustrator and book designer who loves Christmas. She looks forward to colder weather, baking, and decorating her house (and other people's houses, just for fun). You can see more of her work at auroradoesart.com.